Original title:
The Soul's Sacred Stories

Copyright © 2025 Creative Arts Management OÜ
All rights reserved.

Author: Ryan Sterling
ISBN HARDBACK: 978-3-69081-061-6
ISBN PAPERBACK: 978-3-69081-557-4

Ashes of Time

Once I met a dancing ghost,
Tripping over shadows most.
He spilled his tea, the saucer flew,
Said, "Hey, I didn't mean to brew!"

In the attic, I found a hat,
Said it belonged to a pompous cat.
It winked at me, then took a leap,
"I'm late for a nap, don't make me weep!"

We strolled through tales of old,
Where laughter's worth more than gold.
Each sighing whisper held a jest,
Turned every moan into a fest!

Now as we glance through cracks of past,
Life's a hoot, it flies by fast.
In spilt ink, tales are refined,
Every laugh a gem, intertwined.

Tides of Memory and Emotion

Waves of laughter crash ashore,
Every memory we adore.
Sandy feet and silly games,
Singing softly, calling names.

A tidal wave of wacky cheer,
Surfing rumblings, full of beer.
An ocean deep with tales galore,
Shining bright on sandy floor.

A Tapestry of Hidden Journeys

Threads of yarn in colors bright,
Crafting tales that take to flight.
Each stitch tells a joke or two,
Weaves in laughter, never blue.

Unraveled thoughts in tangled thread,
A tapestry of words long said.
Winding paths that twist and turn,
In every loop, we laugh and learn.

The Alchemy of Unseen Threads

Turning gold from simple stones,
Laughs burst forth like silly moans.
Mixing potions of jester's grace,
Turning woes to smiles in space.

Unseen threads that bind us tight,
Spark joy like stars at night.
With giggles, we craft and weave,
In every jest, we find reprieve.

Fables Beneath the Surface

Once upon a time, they say,
Laughter hid in every play.
A fish that danced a funny jig,
And sang of dreams both small and big.

Beneath the waves, they spin and twirl,
With tales that make our senses whirl.
Fables swimming with silly flair,
In every splash, we find our care.

Tapestry of the Spirit

In a corner of my mind, things dance and twirl,
Whispers of wild dreams make my brain whirl.
Tangled tales of cats that wear fancy hats,
And mice that play chess with philosophical spats.

Colors clash and spark with a wink and a jest,
Here lies the place where the oddities rest.
Silly giggles mingle with shadows that race,
As memories flicker like a comical face.

Lament of the Lost

Oh dear me, where did my socks go?
One's in the fridge, the other just won't show!
Perhaps they've run off to a grand sock ball,
Where mismatched pairs waltz, having the best brawl.

Lost tales of hiccups and giggles so sweet,
Each step taken was quite the offbeat.
In the land of the vanished, I bid them all bye,
To continue the quest 'til my pants are too high.

Portraits of a Thousand Lifetimes

Snapshots of laughter in my mind's gallery,
A chicken in sunglasses, it's quite the parody.
Past lives as pirates or interstellar stars,
Each painting a tale that's amusingly bizarre.

From misfit magicians to clumsy old knights,
Juggling with jellybeans in whimsical flights.
I raise my glass to the quirks that unfold,
In the tapestry of memory, hilarious and bold.

Shadows of the Inner World

Within the recesses, shadows tap dance,
Spinning tales of mischief, not left to chance.
A ghost took a selfie and forgot to pose,
While giggling at goblins who wear their old clothes.

Echoes of laughter ring out through the gloom,
With ticklish sensations as outcomes loom.
In this realm of whimsy, we play and we joke,
Crafting our stories in a dance as we poke.

Notes on the Canvas of Time

In a world where clocks laugh, tick-tocking away,
Paint spills laughter, a colorful ballet.
Brush strokes giggle, as colors collide,
Each hue a story, jokes we can't hide.

Doodles of dreams dance on every page,
Time's silly circus, a whimsical stage.
Through whimsical sketches, odd tales unwind,
Each canvas a riddle, mysteries combined.

The rabbits wear watches, quite out of place,
As timelines collide, putting smiles on each face.
With every stroke, our laughter ignites,
In this quirky gallery, the past takes flight.

Reveries from the Depths Within

Beneath the surface, where giggles reside,
Bubbles of nonsense begin to coincide.
Where thoughts wear sombreros, so silly and bright,
In the depths of my mind, there's a carnival light.

A jester named Worry plays tricks in my brain,
He juggles my doubts like they're all just a game.
With each fall and fumble, I chuckle along,
He's dancing in chaos, like he knows he belongs.

In this strange realm, where humor takes flight,
I find that the shadows are not such a fright,
They chuckle as whispers of wisdom appear,
In the depths of my heart, it's all worth a cheer.

Murmurs of the Transcendent Spirit

Whispers from beyond, like a light-hearted breeze,
Tickling the leaves on the tallest of trees.
Spirits in tutu, pirouetting with flair,
Creating a ruckus, floating up in the air.

The echoes of laughter float high like a kite,
As the moon plays peek-a-boo with stars in the night.
The owls share a wink, while the coyotes eye-roll,
In the dance of the cosmos, humor takes its toll.

With a wink and a chuckle, they twirl through the dark,
Painting the night sky with a glimmering spark.
These whispers remind us, in the grand, cosmic play,
Life's a jest, and we're here just to sway.

Aria of the Forgotten Echo

In a hall where the echoes giggle and dance,
Forgotten are stories, lost in a trance.
Voices collide in a melodious hue,
Chasing memories round like a playful zoo.

The ghosts play charades, with no fear of the night,
Their laughter a symphony, a sheer delight.
They flit and they flutter, in costumes so bright,
Staging a comedy, what a peculiar sight!

Each note is a memory, both silly and grand,
While shadows weave tales that are oddly planned.
In the echoes of laughter, I find my own tune,
In this aria of life, where we sing to the moon.

The Dance of Hidden Truths

In the attic, secrets swirl,
Dust bunnies give a twirl.
Old socks tell tales, oh so grand,
Of rogue adventures, unplanned.

A cat winks, eyeing the past,
It knows more than it lets cast.
Invisible treasures in the seams,
Tango with the wildest dreams.

A sandwich, left to age and mold,
Whispers stories, brave and bold.
Each crumb a chapter, full of cheer,
Of meetings with a ghostly deer.

So come and join the silly spree,
Where laughter dances free as can be.
Hidden truths in a silly light,
Underneath the moon's delight.

Fires of Forgotten Legends

In the hearth, the embers glow,
Tales of tricksters, on the go.
A dragon once lost its fiery way,
And turned into a llama's play.

A knight rode with a rubber sword,
In battles fought, he never bored.
With toast and jam, his weapon was,
Against the ogre with sticky paws.

Legends of blunders, mixed with glee,
The queen once danced atop a bee.
Her crown a cake, her scepter bread,
With jellybeans, she ruled instead.

So gather 'round, we roast the past,
With laughter's warmth, the fires cast.
For in these tales of silly strife,
Lies the humor of our life.

Mosaic of Inner Journeys

In a box, my thoughts reside,
Each one winks, none can hide.
Colorful puzzles, bits of fluff,
Words on canvas, never enough.

A journey starts with mismatched shoes,
One size too big, to dance and lose.
With every step, a giggle and flip,
My feet conspire for a wild trip.

With crayons drawn, my mind's a show,
Bright stick figures that steal the glow.
Adventures sketched in rainbow hues,
Chasing giggles, I simply choose.

So here we are, a jumbled mess,
Each piece a story, nothing less.
Together we laugh at this grand spree,
In the mosaic of you and me.

Heartbeats of Time

Tick-tock goes the clock, it's true,
But what if it had a dance to do?
With every chime, a little jig,
Who knew time could be so big?

The minutes hop, they skip and cheer,
While hours lounge, sipping beer.
Seconds chuckle, racing fast,
In the marathon of the past.

Calendars flutter like crazy bats,
As seasons don their silly hats.
Spring tries to tickle winter's nose,
While summer sunbaths in garden rows.

So let's toast to the ticklish rhyme,
Of life's heartbeat, a silly chime.
With laughter echoing through the stream,
We dance along, a funny dream.

Matrices of Meaning

In the dance of daily tasks,
Life juggles joys and flasks.
A cat walks in with sass,
While I ponder the future's class.

Metaphors dressed in silly hats,
Wobble near my curious cats.
While logic trips on rainbow dreams,
Laughter bursts at the seams.

Finding meaning in a sneeze,
A wink, a nod, a gentle tease.
The wisdom's wrapped in bubblegum,
And tickles come without a drum.

In this matrix, truths disguise,
With playful tales and winking eyes.
Every twist gives a hearty chuckle,
As meaning dances, with a shuffle.

Guardians of Hidden Light

In closets filled with dust and socks,
Dwells the keeper of paradox locks.
A ghost stuck in a taco shell,
Whispers secrets that are hard to tell.

With capes made of old bedsheets,
They guard the giggles and messy feats.
Each smile casts a tiny light,
That tickles shadows in the night.

As they sip tea with a mute snail,
Their tales wrap around like a cozy veil.
Giggles echo through the mist,
Of guardians who can't resist.

A flash of light, a splash of fun,
In silly worlds where souls can run.
Magic hides in every wink,
So join the dance, don't overthink!

Remnants of the Unsaid

What's lurking in the spaces bare?
Whispers float without a care.
A chicken crossed but lost its way,
Found truth in laughter's bright ballet.

In the silence where the giggles flee,
Nothing's said but all agree.
A squirrel munches on old regrets,
While the universe plays its safe bets.

Each glance holds a prank, a smile,
We traverse the uncharted aisle.
In the background, silly faces loom,
As unsaid stories fill the room.

In echoes of what could have been,
Laughter bursts, and life begins.
So let's honor what's left unsaid,
With chuckles that dance in our head.

Flashes of the Inner Universe

In my brain, stars collide and fuse,
With thoughts dancing in mismatched shoes.
A comet zips past a broccoli,
While gravity thinks it's quite folly.

Galactic giggles swirl around,
In bouncing thoughts, they can be found.
Each idea wears a silly grin,
As it spins out from deep within.

With a wink, my neurons play,
In this cosmic cabaret display.
Here's a jungle gym made of dreams,
Where nothing's ever as it seems.

Flashes of joy, a wink of fate,
Collaborate as they levitate.
In this universe of delight,
We laugh aloud, embracing the night.

Cracked Mirrors and Light

In a mirror cracked and bright,
Reflections dance with sheer delight.
A winking grin, a silly face,
Each shard a tale, a funny place.

Fractured thoughts that twist and twirl,
Like a clown's antics in a whirl.
They wink at life with a cheeky cheer,
To remind us all to never fear.

With each glance, a giggle grows,
The comedy of life, it surely shows.
In every crack a laughter's brew,
A sparkling hint of something new.

So let us laugh at what we find,
In broken bits, joy intertwined.
For every mirror's funny twist,
Holds stories that we can't resist.

The Breath of Ancient Voices

In echo chambers of the past,
Whispers linger, laughter cast.
Voices giggle in the breeze,
Echoing through the ancient trees.

"Did you hear?" one spirit said,
"I once tripped over my own thread!"
Laughter bubbles from the ground,
Ancient jesters, oh what a sound!

With every breath, a tale awakes,
Like silly pranks and funny fakes.
They barter jokes along the wind,
Each punchline a new story pinned.

So listen close when silence falls,
To laughter hidden in the walls.
For ancient voices share their whims,
With every breeze, joy simply swims.

Celestial Cartography

Mapping stars with giggles bright,
Constellations fold in light.
Dancing planets, silly shapes,
As each one antics, joy escapes.

A comet's tail, a joke so grand,
With laughter tossed across the land.
The Milky Way, a twisty line,
Crafted by a cosmic design.

"Oh look!" the moon pokes fun,
"Do you think these stars are done?"
While stardust twinkles, sly and sweet,
Their humor makes the night complete.

So chart your path among the gleams,
With humor stitched into your dreams.
For in the cosmos, funny we find,
A playful dance, both bright and kind.

Labyrinths of Emotion

In mazes deep where feelings spin,
Emotions laugh, they always win.
Joy and sorrow, a tangled thread,
Each turn unveils what's left unsaid.

A twist of glee, a cornered frown,
As laughter spins the world around.
Was that a giggle or a sigh?
In this labyrinth, both fly high.

With every step, a joke appears,
To tickle softly at our fears.
Anxiety trips on a playful jest,
Finding humor in life's quest.

So wander through with lightened heart,
In every corner, find your part.
For in this maze of silly plight,
Lurks laughter, ready to ignite.

Starborn Stories

In a sky of glowing stars,
A cat in a spaceship plays guitars.
Singing tunes of cosmic glee,
While squirrels dance on Mars with tea.

Aliens laugh at Earthly ways,
Their humor stretches across the rays.
Trading jokes for spacey snacks,
Giggles echo through the cracks.

A comet zips with a prankster's flair,
Kicking up stardust everywhere.
Belts of asteroids chuckle bright,
In the vast expanse of silly flight.

So when the night is dressed in black,
Remember the laughter on the track.
For in the universe, fun is the key,
With tales as wild as you and me.

The Confluence of Dreams

In a land where pillows float so high,
Snoring dragons patch the sky.
Clouds made of cotton candy drift,
As dreams and giggles take a lift.

A rabbit in a waistcoat spins,
Telling tales of fluffy wins.
While goldfish debate the best of shows,
With popcorn served from tiny toes.

Pineapple clouds rain juicy drops,
While caterpillars breakdance in flops.
Every dream is a comical ride,
With laughter bouncing on the tide.

So dive into dreams both wild and fun,
Where every mischief is just begun.
Stand tall on clouds, let your worries fly,
In the dizzy dance of a starry sky.

Nurtured by Nostalgia

Old photographs turn into pets,
With memories dressed in silly debts.
Grandpa's jokes still echo clear,
As we laugh at his ancient gear.

Toys from the past come out to play,
Each one has something funny to say.
Rubber ducks and action guys,
Wielding crayon swords and sweet surprise.

Mom's old recipes come alive,
Gooey cakes with strange ingredients thrive.
We bake in chaos, flour on the floor,
In the kitchen, laughter's the core!

So let's toast to tales that never grow old,
With giggles and memories bright and bold.
For in nostalgia's warm embrace,
We find the joy in every face.

Pathways of Perception

On the road of thought, I tripped on a shoe,
An odd little left made the right one rue.
With a laugh at my feet, I danced with a tree,
Who giggled and swayed, just as clever as me.

Through squiggly paths where the grass talks back,
I met a wise snail with a tiny backpack.
He shared silly secrets of the earth's great goop,
And laughed as we formed a wiggly troop.

Clouds dripping wisdom in puddles of fun,
Where thinking takes flight like a whimsical run.
Every detour leads to a quirky delight,
As we chase after giggles that take flight.

So come dance with me on this strange, funny road,
Where perception is joy and laughter is bestowed.
For in this journey of curious views,
Every step is a laugh, and each thought is a muse.

Songs from the Depths

In the depths where laughter dwells,
Silly fish weave funny spells.
Octopuses dance with glee,
Singing tunes beneath the sea.

Crabs pull pranks and tickle toes,
Bubbling jokes and belly woes.
Sea turtles join a conga line,
As jellyfish sway, looking divine.

Starfish laugh at sunbathing men,
Poking fun again and again.
With each wave a joke is told,
Ocean's humor, bright and bold.

So when you dive into the blue,
Remember, the ocean laughs too!
With each splash a chuckle invades,
Songs from depths where laughter parades.

Ink of the Immortal

In the quill of time, I scribble vast,
On ancient scrolls, I leave my cast.
With ink that shimmers, giggles arise,
Every stroke is a prank in disguise.

The scribes chuckle at words they trace,
As I swap their names in a wild race.
"Oh, look!" says one, "I'm now a queen!"
"Or maybe a duck?" with giggle unseen.

Scrolls of old have secrets, too,
With tales of mishaps and a shoe.
Wizards drop potions, giggling loud,
While fairies spin jokes in a cloud.

So read the lines with a playful heart,
For every tale has its funny part.
Ink the immortal, forever bold,
Whispers of laughter from ages old.

Veils of Yesterday

Behind veils where shadows play,
Lies a jester's game of yesterday.
Wacky hats and shoes askew,
Unravel tales, both old and new.

Grandma's stories, quite absurd,
Of talking cats and flying birds.
With every twist, a wink is shared,
In giggles, we find the truth unpaired.

Echoes of laughter dance through time,
A clown's mischief, a rhythm and rhyme.
As veils lift to reveal the past,
Each tale is a joke meant to last.

When you peek behind what has been,
Find humor in the places unseen.
Veils of yesterday, light and cheery,
Sprinkled with laughter, never dreary.

Collecting Moments

In a jar, I store bright days,
With giggles twinkling in sun's rays.
Butterflies, pebbles, and laughter loud,
Moments collected, unbowed and proud.

A sunny patch or rainy gloom,
Each little giggle makes joy bloom.
With everyday wonders held so tight,
My jar gets fuller by each night.

Silly faces and funny vows,
A penguin wearing giant bows.
In moments shared, we find the spark,
Of humor brightening up the dark.

So gather your moments, sticky sweet,
With every laugh, make life complete.
Collecting moments, a merry dance,
In jars of joy, give life a chance.

The Heart's Celestial Script

In the cosmos of my chest, a dance so bright,
Each beat a giggle, stars twinkling light.
Jokes etched in stardust, I hold dear,
My heart's a stand-up, it's quite the weird!

Whispers of mischief, the sun's winking jest,
An eclipse of chuckles, it never rests.
Asteroids of laughter, orbit my mind,
In this playful universe, blissfully blind.

Galactic tickles that never fade,
Meteor showers where punchlines are laid.
Constellations giggling in perfect tune,
As my heart scribbles stories under the moon.

Riddles of the Inner Landscape

Within my mind, a maze of quirks,
Riddles popping up like playful jerks.
The trees gossip with their leaves in flight,
Squirrels cracking jokes from morning to night.

Clouds float by, sharing sly remarks,
Dancing shadows, giving life to sparks.
A brook chuckles under pebbles so small,
Ripples of humor in its merry call.

Mountains of laughter, valleys so bright,
Echoes of giggles create pure delight.
Every corner holds a punchline unsaid,
In this inner playground, joy is widespread.

Threads of an Infinite Narrative

Weaving tales with colors galore,
Each stitch a chuckle, who could ask for more?
Knots of wonder, tangled with glee,
Threads of laughter, stitching a spree.

Unraveling yarns, the cat gives chase,
As I spin fables, a most curious race.
Each twist and turn holds a goofy surprise,
Humor embedded in tales that rise.

Quilted dreams, a patchwork parade,
The fabric of fun, no rules to invade.
In this endless narrative, joy takes the lead,
Sewn together by giggles, we all shall succeed.

Harmonies of the Stillness Within

In silence, I chuckle at thoughts gone astray,
Harmonizing giggles, oh what a display!
The calmness sings with a warm, silly tone,
Whispers of joy in a quiet cyclone.

Between each heartbeat, a joke takes flight,
Stillness croons tunes of delight in the night.
Serenity dances, a waltz oh so fair,
While laughter tiptoes through the wisps of air.

Melodies shimmer like stars in a dream,
The peace of the moment is bursting at the seam.
In this tranquil bubble, fun resonates,
As the echoes of joy open heart's gates.

Tides of Thought

My mind's a beach, oh what a sight,
Waves crash in with all their might.
Some thoughts float like beach balls bright,
While others sink, oh what a fright!

Seagulls squawk, they steal my fries,
Like pesky thoughts, they catch you by surprise.
A tidal wave of jokes that rise,
Leaves me giggling 'neath the skies.

Sandy castles made from dreams,
Wobbly towers, bursting at the seams.
Each grain of thought, or so it seems,
A story shared in silly themes.

So ride the surf, don't miss the fun,
With whimsy, life's a vibrant pun.
The tides of thought will always run,
In this mad world, we've just begun!

Souls Unfolding

I met a cloud, he wore a grin,
Said, 'Life's a race, let's begin!'
He tossed me thoughts, oh what a din,
Like butterflies that sip on gin!

We laughed at stars who lost their way,
Trailed by giggles, night and day.
Each secret shared, a grand ballet,
In chaos bright, we chose to stay.

With every fold of cosmic dreams,
A bag of chips, or so it seems.
We danced in socks, with silly themes,
Oh, to be part of laughter's beams!

So venture forth, don't wear a frown,
In stories shared, we won't back down.
With every turn, we'll wear the crown,
In absurd tales, there's no renown!

Gardens of Reflective Stories

In gardens green, where thoughts take root,
I plant my quirks like veggies cute.
Some sprout up high, others in pursuit,
Of sunlight, laughter, and a funny flute!

The bunnies hop, they tell their jokes,
While daisies giggle, not for folks.
With every bloom, more laughter evokes,
Their dance is wild, the wind just chokes.

Underneath the sun, my mind expands,
Chasing shadows with silly hands.
Each flower's tale, like whispered bands,
We celebrate life, with goofy stands.

So wander here, through colors bright,
In every petal, find delight.
With tales to share, our hearts take flight,
In gardens where we bask in light!

Refuge in Recollection

I found a chest, dusty and old,
Full of memories, worth their weight in gold.
Each trinket a tale, so weirdly bold,
Like the day I wore socks in the cold!

My grandma's laugh echoes in my mind,
With every story, new joy I find.
Her jokes, like candy, are sweetly unlined,
In this refuge, I'm endlessly entwined.

With photographs that dance and sway,
In every corner, they come to play.
Old socks and tales, a true cabaret,
We laugh til dawn, then dream away.

So dive in deep, let laughter reign,
In memories' arms, there's no more pain.
Each silly moment, bright as a train,
In recollection's joy, we'll dance again!

Beneath the Stars of Human Experience

Under the sky where wishes float,
A cat in a hat, striking a pose.
A squirrel rides bikes, oh what a joke,
Chasing its tail right where it goes.

Pigeons discussing their latest flight,
Comparing their styles, who flies the best?
While ants in a conga line search for delight,
As cookies crumble, they truly rest.

A dog tells tales of his mighty chase,
As the mailman hides behind a tree.
With each wagging tale, he sets the pace,
Making us laugh with glee and spree.

Beneath the stars, we jest and play,
Life's silly moments we can't ignore.
Every heart holds a giggle to sway,
Unraveling joy forevermore.

Shards of Light in Twilight

In twilight's glow, the fridge spins tales,
Of snacks that vanish like fairy dust.
Leftovers whining, their fate it pales,
While pickles dance to a funky bust.

A tea bag sings with a wobbly tune,
As the kettle starts to groove and sway.
With every boil, it reaches the moon,
And spills its secrets at end of day.

Candles gossip about waxy dreams,
Flames flicker while sharing their loot.
They drip and drop in laughter streams,
Creating art that's almost a hoot.

Under the canvas of fading light,
Giggles echo, a delightful sound.
In life's absurdity, all feels right,
Amidst the chaos, joy's always found.

Vignettes from the Heart's Treasure

In a drawer of memories, socks have a chat,
On why they lose their partners so fast.
With stories of lint and a bold cat,
They ponder the fate of their woven past.

A rubber band stretches its tales with pride,
Of how it catapulted across the room.
While a button frets from being untied,
Sighing of seams that led to their doom.

Old photographs laugh with each dim glance,
Sharing whispers of days filled with cheer.
The moments captured lead to a dance,
As each figure twirls away from the fear.

Vignettes emerge from the heart's deep chest,
Every giggle, a small flare of light.
In this treasure, we are truly blessed,
For laughter sings, banishing the night.

A Tidal Wave of Unspoken Truths

A tidal wave of thoughts brews inside,
As jellybeans argue on flavor reign.
With peppermint dreams that can't abide,
As a cookie grumbles for some refraine.

While shoes, mismatched, engage in a race,
Competing to trip over the rainbow's end.
The rules seem silly, but who can replace
The laughter birthed when clumsy things bend?

Clouds share secrets of storms up ahead,
As raindrops giggle racing down a leaf.
While thunder chuckles from its own bed,
Bringing us moments of sweet disbelief.

In this wave of whimsical thoughts untold,
Every truth wrapped in chuckles and cheer.
From silly mishaps to tales of old,
Life's laughter echoes when we draw near.

Mysteries of Existence

Why do socks always go missing,
While my cat keeps on pissing?
Is the universe playing a prank,
Or does my laundry have a secret bank?

I ponder life's grand design,
Over coffee and donuts, feeling fine.
Perhaps there's a cosmic joke we miss,
Wrapped in the fabric of endless abyss.

The stars blink and wink their light,
While I trip over my dog's delight.
What tales do the galaxies hide,
When all I find is my ego's pride?

So laugh with me at this cosmic jest,
For in humor, we find the best.
In every twist, in every turn,
There's wisdom hidden, waiting to learn.

The Language of Unseen Worlds

If ghosts could text, what would they say?
"Hey, seen the remote? It's gone astray!"
Do they gossip in the evening air,
About our blunders and epic despair?

Whispers of worlds we cannot see,
Might just be cats faking a plea.
"Feed us more, we're not just fluff,"
In the game of life, they call every bluff.

Perhaps aliens laugh at our plight,
While watching us dine like it's a fight.
Do they shake their heads at our silly dreams,
Or join us for snacks and laugh at our schemes?

In this cosmos of laughter and fun,
Even silence can be a good pun.
So let's raise a toast to voices unheard,
In joy and folly, let laughter be stirred!

Dance of Eternal Echoes

Every footstep on the floor is a dance,
A chance to twirl, a moment to prance.
But watch out for that rogue chair leg,
It might trip you up, like an unseen peg!

Echoes bounce off the walls and sing,
Of mishaps and trips that make hearts spring.
I slip on a banana, thankfully soft,
And suddenly, I'm the star, a goofball aloft.

Infinity shimmies in a comical spin,
Every laugh adds to the double chinned grin.
Is the universe choreographing our moves?
Or is it just us being silly with grooves?

Laughter enhances this cosmic ballet,
As shadows waltz in a joking display.
In this theater where humor ignites,
Even the echoes join in for bites!

Secrets of the Silent Shore

I walked along the shore so bare,
Sandy toes, wind-tangled hair.
What secrets do the waves convey,
Beside my beach towel in disarray?

Every shell a silent gossip spree,
Revealing tales of the deep blue sea.
"Dude, waves came crashing last night,
Told us about your epic moonlit flight!"

We giggle at crabs doing the hustle,
While seagulls squawk and cause a tussle.
What wisdom lies under the tide?
Or are they just fish trying to hide?

So let's embrace this sandy delight,
With laughter that echoes into the night.
At the silent shore of jokes untold,
We'll find treasures, both funny and bold.

Dreamscapes of Existence

In dreams I ride on rainbow beams,
With marshmallow clouds and chocolate streams.
Moonlight laughs, it tickles my nose,
Chasing shadows while everyone doze.

A cat in a hat spins a yarn so grand,
While dancing penguins take the stand.
We toast with juice from coconuts bright,
In this wacky world, it just feels right.

Silly thoughts like bubbles do float,
On banana boats that don't need a coat.
The chuckling stars play hide and seek,
In giggling glades, we laugh and peek.

Oh, what a ride through this whimsical space,
Where time trips over its own shoelace.
With every chuckle, the heart grows wide,
In these dreamscapes where dreams collide.

Radiant Tales of the Journeyed Heart

Once I packed my bags with glee,
Filled with sunshine and extra tea.
My socks mismatched like a clown's parade,
On paths of laughter, the joy won't fade.

I met a frog with quite the stance,
Wearing glasses in a jazzy dance.
He croaked the tunes of silly lore,
Inviting me to hop and explore.

With every step, the stories burst,
Like fizzy drinks, we quenched our thirst.
A twirl, a spin, a jump so high,
We painted rainbows across the sky.

Oh, these tales, they shimmer and sway,
Under the laughter of a silly day.
Each heartbeat plays a catchy tune,
In radiant dreams beneath the moon.

Whispers of the Heart

Whispers tickle like butterflies,
In the garden of giggles, where laughter flies.
A tiny mouse in a jacket of thread,
Dancing with daisies, all worries shed.

The clock strikes silly, it's time to play,
With jellybeans bouncing, come what may.
Each whisper a tickle, a chuckle, a grin,
In heart's gentle corners, let the fun begin.

Voices croon from the clouds up high,
As silly squirrels let out a sigh.
Tales of nonsense flutter and roam,
In the cozy crannies we call our home.

From buried treasure to chocolate streams,
This heart's a canvas of giggling dreams.
In whispers soft, we find our song,
In the humor of life, we all belong.

Ocean of Memories

The sea's a wavy, giggly friend,
With whispers of laughter that never end.
Turtles wear shades and surf on the foam,
In this ocean of memories, we find our home.

Shrimp in tuxedos dance on the shore,
While jellyfish waltz, craving encore.
Together we splash with a splash of cheer,
In this salty realm, there's nothing to fear.

Waves tell tales of moonlit zests,
With sandcastles wearing their finest vests.
Starfish giggle at tales untold,
As crabs pull pranks, fiercely bold.

From seashells bright to treasure chests,
This ocean of laughter surely invests.
In every ripple, a memory flows,
In the heart's deep depths, the joy only grows.

Chronicles of the Unsung Essence

In a pickle jar, dreams collide,
A pizza slice, where hopes abide.
With cats that dance and mice that sing,
Life's a circus, with a funny fling.

In grandma's hat, we share a joke,
The world a stage, where we all poke.
With socks on hands and shoes on heads,
We ponder truths, as laughter spreads.

Beneath the stars, we play charades,
With crayons bright, we draw parades.
Each chuckle sparks a brand-new fight,
In jest, we find our endless light.

So here's to tales, both weird and wild,
In our joyful chaos, we're all just children.
The essence of life, with all its flair,
A comedy club, with love to share.

Light Beyond the Veil

A banana peel, a slip, a grin,
Underneath the laughter, we begin.
With silly hats and socks askew,
In a birthday bash for a kangaroo.

Whispers ride the air like kites,
Chasing shadows in funny fights.
A giraffe with shades and a polka-dot tie,
Making us giggle as it strolls by.

A tumble down the grassy hill,
With every roll, we feel the thrill.
The stars above twinkle and tease,
While we bump our heads on the trees.

So let's dance like nobody cares,
With painted toes, we'll do our dares.
In the veil of laughter, we'll find our way,
With light hearts singing, come what may.

Memoirs of a Dreamer's Dawn

With pancakes flying, dreams take off,
A toaster sings, we break and scoff.
In slippers big, we face the day,
Chasing clouds that drift away.

Sunshine peeks through curtains drawn,
We laugh as we dance on the lawn.
With jokes that flip like pancakes fried,
In dreams we find our hearts collide.

A turtle in a race, oh my!
As we cheer loud, it waves goodbye.
With every giggle and silly grin,
The dreamer stirs, let the fun begin!

So raise a toast to the dawn's delight,
With laughter echoing through the night.
In every dream, let joy abound,
As we spin tales like merry-go-rounds.

Gifts from the Whispering Wind

A whisper stirs, it dances near,
With tickles and chuckles, we hold dear.
Kites take flight on a gusty day,
As clouds blow kisses, they skip away.

With scarves that flutter in a grand ballet,
The wind confides in a cheeky sway.
Each tale it shares brings giggles and sighs,
As we chase rainbows in the skies.

A tumbleweed rolls with a grin so wide,
Riding the breeze on a whimsical ride.
Between the giggles and breezy bends,
Is where true magic always descends.

So let's unravel the whispers loud,
With every smile, let dreams be proud.
In the dance of the wind, we find our tune,
As laughter fills the afternoon.

Echoes in the Silence

In a world where whispers play,
A butterfly forgot its way.
It landed on a cat's soft nose,
Surprised, it sneezed, and off it goes!

A tree once tried to join the dance,
But got its roots caught in romance.
With branches waving to the beat,
It fell, and still pretended to be neat!

A cloud that fancied itself a hat,
Sat on a turtle, imagine that!
The turtle grinned, 'What a fine prize!'
But rain fell down, surprising the skies!

To think the silence speaks so loud,
With giggles hiding in the crowd.
Echoes hold their breath and pause,
As laughter waits without a cause.

Threads of Existence

Life's a quilt with threads unspooled,
Each stitch a laugh, all hope renewed.
A wise old shoe once said with glee,
'I'm not just worn, I'm full of spree!'

A sock conspirator took a stand,
With missing mates, it formed a band.
They sang of laundry days so bright,
And danced around in pure delight!

A button jumped off for a stroll,
To find its way to a dinner roll.
It rolled and bounced with charming flair,
'This bread's the place for button wear!'

Threads weave tales both wild and funny,
With every misstep, there's bright honey.
In each loose end, more laughs are found,
As life's strange stitches spin around.

Dreams Woven in Starlight

Once a dream dashed off in fright,
Chased by shadows under starlight.
It tripped and fell in moonlit streams,
Splashing around in giggling beams!

A wish wished hard upon a star,
But missed its mark and flew too far.
It landed on a sleeping bear,
Who snorted loud, then tossed in air!

In slumber's grasp, the dreams engage,
With wacky plots that fill the page.
They mix and mingle, plot their schemes,
Creating chaos in our dreams!

So when the night whispers your name,
Know every dream's a wild game.
They dance and twist, laugh and shout,
Under the stars, without a doubt!

Chronicles of the Unseen

In realms where giggles hide away,
Invisible friends come out to play.
They play hopscotch on the breeze,
And laugh at humans with such ease!

A poltergeist on a kitchen spree,
Made cookies dance, oh, what a sight to see!
With flour flies and rolling pins,
They served the ghosts some frosted sins!

The moonlit night held secrets grand,
Where shadows formed a marching band.
They serenaded with their zest,
Making mischief, never a rest!

Chronicles penned in laughter's light,
Fill pages with joy, oh what a sight!
In unseen tales, we find our glee,
The funny paths of mystery!

The Luminescence of Hidden Paths

In a world of lost umbrellas,
Twinkling dreams chase playful fables.
Cats wear hats and dance on roofs,
While socks escape in giggling gables.

Moonbeams laugh at sleepy stars,
As time trips over shoelace knots.
A toaster plays the ukulele,
While toast debates if butter's hot.

Giggles echo through the trees,
Where shadows wear mismatched shoes.
Ballet dancing in the rain,
Stumbling, oh, what silly blues!

With each quirk and quirky twist,
The wind whispers tales of fun.
Life's a jest, take heart and smile,
Hidden paths are never done.

Reflections in the Mirror of Being

In the mirror, a fish can sing,
While chairs gossip about the rug.
Dogs debate the meaning of life,
As pepper shakers dance a shrug.

Candles argue on the shelf,
About whose flame burns the brightest.
The clock giggles every hour,
Tick-tock, not quite the slightest!

A penguin winks at passing pride,
Sipping tea in a polka dot hat.
Mirror reflections tell us tales,
About where we've been, and that!

Through laughter and silly spins,
We find our truths in playful grace.
Life's a dance, an opera slight,
With smiles and laughter as its base.

Serendipity's Silent Song

In the pantry, marshmallows scheme,
To launch a rocket made of cream.
Pickles dream of jazz and swing,
While donuts hum a cheerful theme.

A squirrel in a tuxedo prances,
While spaghetti serenades the bread.
Unsaid tales weave through the air,
As jolly whispers spark ahead.

Cucumbers tango in the fridge,
Charming lonely jars of jam.
With each step, a silly twirl,
Life's a rhyme, a bursting slam!

Each chance encounter yields a laugh,
A hiccup turns to joy divine.
In the melody of life we find,
The sweetest notes through every line.

Journeys Through the Ether

A spaceship made of spaghetti flies,
Past planets adorned with waffles fine.
The stars throw pancakes down to Earth,
While aliens dine on fizzy brine.

On cloud nine, a giraffe plays chess,
Challenging squirrels for grand delight.
Balloons hold debates about dreams,
While skippy clouds glow soft and bright.

A rocket skids on rainbow trails,
Chasing comet tails that giggle loud.
Journeying through the whims of space,
In cosmic puns, we're all endowed.

Through every twist and bubble thrill,
We find joy beneath starlit skies.
Dancing through the cosmic game,
Laughter's the map that always flies.

Rhythms of an Ancient Heartbeat

In a land where the old folks dance,
Their knees creak with every chance.
They tell tales of love gone wrong,
While munching cookies and singing a song.

Beneath the moon, a cat did prance,
Spilling secrets with every glance.
The owls chuckle, the frogs will croak,
As grandpa sneezes, the whole place chokes.

Wizards in hats full of yarn,
Dreaming of when they were born.
They argue 'bout socks and shoes that don't fit,
While ghosts of past come out to knit.

A squirrel tried to join the fun,
His tales of acorns, not a ton.
The heartbeat of laughter, a rhythm divine,
Echoes of humor that twist and entwine.

Threads Connecting Generations

In grandma's quilt, stories unfold,
Each patch a memory, glittering gold.
With knots that bind, and stitches galore,
Laughter in threads, we always want more.

Tales from the past, stitched with delight,
Of how grandpa danced all night.
He slipped on his foot and fell with a curl,
While grandma just laughed and gave it a whirl.

Naps get interrupted by giggles at play,
As cousins exchange the best stories each day.
With marshmallows toastin' in s'mores by the fire,
Where secrets get shared and stories inspire.

So gather the young and the old near the flame,
Where threads of connection are never the same.
With humor and love, we weave and we spin,
Creating a tapestry where all can begin.

Fireside Tales of the Spirit

Gather around, the fire's aglow,
With marshmallow sticks, we're ready to go.
Uncle Joe starts with a tale from his youth,
'Bout a ghost with a shoe that was missing a tooth.

The flames flicker, shadows dance wild,
While cousins giggle, each one a child.
A monster that ate the last piece of cake,
Or maybe it was just a sleepy mistake?

Each story gets taller, more outlandish,
With dragons and wizards, the odds are quite Spanish.
They laugh 'bout their fears, the shadows of night,
While roasting some weenies, a true delight.

So let's toast to our fears, our hilarities too,
For fireside tales bring the old into view.
With sparks in the air and laughter to share,
Every heartbeat connects us— a spirit laid bare!

Whispered Remnants of Being

In the attic, dusty treasures lie,
Whispers of dreams that flutter and fly.
A record player plays tunes from the past,
While grandma twirls by, memories amassed.

Old letters, like butterflies trapped in time,
Page after page, the laughter, the rhyme.
With silly nicknames and jokes that we bold,
Tales from the family, all sweet and gold.

A rocking chair creaks with rhythm of days,
As stories of mishaps spin in a haze.
Like Aunt Mildred's hat, too big for her head,
Or cousin Jake's beard that no one had fed.

In corners they whisper, reminders so sly,
Of love and of laughter, we can't say goodbye.
The remnants of moments, crisp as a dream,
Woven together, they dance and they beam.

Stillness Beneath the Surface

In a pond that's not too deep,
A frog once jumped to take a leap.
But instead of a splash he found a seat,
On a lily pad, so soft and sweet.

The fish below, they stared in shock,
As he grinned and rocked, it's quite the mock.
"I'm the king of naps on this lily top,
While you all swim, I'll never swap!"

A turtle then peeked with a wise grin tight,
Said, "You think you're cool, but look at my height!"
And off he went with a graceful glide,
While the frog just rested, feeling quite proud inside.

So if life feels tough or full of strife,
Just remember the frog and his lazy life.
Sometimes stillness is where we find our cheer,
Even if it's a little weird, let's all give a cheer.

Lanterns in the Dark

One night a mouse took a little stroll,
With a lantern that he found, feeling quite whole.
He tripped on a cat, who was trying to sneak,
And they both shouted, 'Oh! This is quite the peak!'

The mouse held his lantern, a flickering spark,
While the cat just blinked in the cold, dark park.
"Why do you need light? You're supposed to be sly!"
Squeaked the little mouse up to the night sky.

But the cat held her paw with a flick and a flare,
"Even hunters need light, isn't that fair?"
They laughed and they danced 'neath the moon's soft glow,
Two pals in the night, giving friendship a show.

So if you find darkness around your own way,
Remember that laughter can brighten the gray.
Like a mouse and a cat, let your worries depart,
And shine like the lanterns—you're a true work of art!

Reflections of Ancient Wisdom

In a garden of veggies, a wise old sage,
Whispered to carrots, both funny and sage.
"Listen here, sprouts, you're more than your roots,
Dance in the rain, and wear your rain boots!"

The beets got a chuckle, 'Who needs to grow tall?
We'd rather be short, and eat snacks at the mall!'
With a wink and a nod, they had fun in the mud,
While the sage sipped tea, all happy and snug.

So the daisies chimed in, with petals aflutter,
"Why not embrace this, oh, garden of butter?"
With laughter and joy, they all twirled around,
In a patch of silliness, wisdom was found.

So take heed, dear friends, when life seems a bore,
Just plant the seeds of laughter and more.
A veggie brigade, so funny and wise,
Will surely sprout joy, right before your eyes!

The Alchemy of Experience

A squirrel named Nutsy had quite the career,
He'd gather his acorns and hoard them with cheer.
One day in a frenzy, he forgot where they lay,
And laughed, looking up at the clouds, 'What a day!'

He tried to impress with his stories of old,
But the tales turned to laughter, quite goofy and bold.
"I once stole a cookie from a picnicking crew,
But slipped on a blanket, and screamed—'Who knew?'"

His pals rolled with giggles, their sides all a-splitting,
As Nutsy recounted each misstep, admitting.
In the end they agreed, with twinkles in eyes,
That learning through laughter is the best kind of prize.

So when you feel lost, like a nut with no way,
Just chuckle and wink—embrace every day.
The art of experience can bring joy and glee,
With a squirrel leading laughter—oh, can't you see?

Spiral Pathways of the Heart

In a world quite absurd, we spin and twirl,
Chasing dreams like a cat chasing her pearl.
With each winding turn, we giggle and sigh,
For love's little quirks make us laugh till we cry.

We stumble and bumble, oh what a dance,
Two left feet in rhythm, a comical prance.
With a heart full of whimsy, we glide and we swoon,
Even when life feels like a wacky cartoon.

Each heartbeat's a joke, with a punchline so fine,
Tickling fates with a sip of cheap wine.
As we waltz through our blunders, we learn to embrace,
That humor's the glue in this comical race.

So let's toast to the fumbles, the flops, and the fun,
For love's a grand circus, and we've just begun.
With every misstep, we laugh on the way,
For the heart's winding pathways lead us to play.

A Canvas of Unconfined Thoughts

With colors of nonsense, I paint my mind bright,
Each stroke a giggle, each splash pure delight.
Oh, to be free like a bird in a hat,
Flapping around like a splattered-up cat!

From doodles to daydreams, I scribble and scheme,
Creating a canvas of whimsical dreams.
With thoughts like balloons that float up and away,
I chase after laughter—what else can I say?

There's chaos in colors, a ruckus in paint,
Each brush a calamity, oh, how quaint!
Yet hidden in madness, a spark often springs,
A tickle in brain that just giggles and sings.

So let's scatter our joys, like confetti on air,
In this wild art journey, we haven't a care.
For in every mishap, there's magic afoot,
It's the quirks of our thoughts that truly uproot!

Collisions of Fate and Free Will

Oh fate, you silly, mischievous chap,
Dancing with free will in a boisterous clap!
Like pancakes and syrup, you stick and you flip,
In this kitchen of chaos, you just can't grip!

We tango and tangle in a dizzying show,
With choices like confetti, all scattered to throw.
Each decision a drama, a game of charades,
While fate rolls its eyes at the mess we've made.

We're puppets on strings, oh what a delight,
In the circus of choices, we twirl left and right.
With a wink and a nudge, we tumble and spin,
As fate gives a chuckle, "Where have you been?"

So here's to the clowns in this great cosmic play,
Where options collide in a comical way.
For it's laughter that lights up each twist and each bend,
In the dance of our lives on this wild, funny trend.

Echoing Dreams of the Past

In echoes of yesterday, we grin and we guffaw,
At those bright, silly moments; oh, what a flaw!
When hairdos were tragic and fashion a joke,
We laughed 'til the tears came, then nearly broke.

Oh, those dreams were a riot, with quirks grand and bold,
As we stumbled through life wearing mismatched gold.
We chased after fairies and fanciful schemes,
In a world of our making, we lived out our dreams.

With each silly face from those years long gone by,
We chuckle at moments that make us ask why!
For the laughter of youth, it still tickles our insides,
As we trip down memory lane on whimsical rides.

So let's raise a glass to the past that we shared,
To those echoing dreams that had everyone scared.
For in silly remembrance, we find a sweet heart,
In the tapestry woven, where the laughter's the art.

Elysium in Everyday Life

In the kitchen, I dance with a spoon,
The cat joins in, a furry cartoon.
Eggs are flying, what a sight,
Breakfast battles turn into delight!

Neighbors peek through the window wide,
Wondering where my rhythm hides.
They laugh, they point, I give a twirl,
Spatula high, I'm ready to unfurl!

The dishes pile with a clatter and crash,
While I juggle pans, a kitchen bash.
Laughter echoes, my heart takes flight,
In this chaos, everything feels right!

So here in the mundane, I find my glee,
In every slip and pancake spree.
Elysium waits in silly design,
In everyday life, the magic is mine!

Heartstrings of Time

A clock in the hall sings a silly tune,
Tick-tock, tick-tock, it's a little loony.
It laughs at my plans, always runs late,
Time's a trickster, it can be great!

Old photos slip from dusty frames,
Faces smile with unfashionable names.
I giggle at hairdos gone far awry,
A fashion faux pas that makes me sigh!

Grandma's tales twist like a rubber band,
She swears that penguins can dance on land.
With every story, my heartstrings hum,
The more absurd, the better the fun!

In the garden, we chase the breeze,
Playing tag with the bumblebees.
With laughter echoing, we watch birds mime,
In the heartstrings of days gone by, we climb!

The Unfolding of Memories

Memories unfold like a creaky drawer,
Every paper's a tale, who could ask for more?
Beneath crumpled maps and forgotten plans,
Are toy soldiers and glittery bands!

A post-it note reminding me to play,
With a smiley face, 'You're okay!'
Childhood whispers dance through the air,
As I pull out a cupcake tin, with flair!

Laughter spills from each silly note,
Some poems written on a cereal box coat.
Every crayon scrawl tells a truth,
From daily antics of long-lost youth.

In this trove of giggles, secrets abound,
Each memory wrapped in a frosty surround.
I treasure the absurd, it's a joyful spin,
In the unfolding of laughter, life begins!

Mists of Forgotten Roads

Down the lane where memories play,
The past is silly, come what may.
Mists roll in like a clumsy friend,
Hiding the paths where laughter bends.

I trip on a stone that looks like a shoe,
And laugh at the tales it could construe.
Each bump on the way, a jest in disguise,
The journey unfolds with comic surprise!

Every corner is bursting with quirks,
Where squirrels in tutus do funny jerks.
I chase after rainbows with a giggle,
In the mists of the past, I take a wiggle!

So let the forgotten roads reveal,
The joy in the silly, the whimsical feel.
In every stumble and every cheer,
The mists remind us—fun's always near!

Harbor of Past Lives

In a port where memories dance,
Old ships whisper tales of chance.
Pirates argue, hands on hips,
About treasure and their silly trips.

A sailor claims he sailed to Mars,
While picking fights with cranky stars.
His ship was made of bacon,

But nobody's sure what he's forsaken.

A mermaid laughs, she's got a tail,
Says, "I just swam to the ice cream trail!"
Yet every scoop leaves her in a spin,
For there's always a fish with a cheeky grin.

So, dock your boat by the sandy shore,
Catch a wave and then explore.
In this harbor, lives collide with glee,
Chasing laughter 'neath the olive trees.

Treasure Maps of the Heart

With a crumpled map tucked in my vest,
I seek the 'X' to put love to the test.
Cross a bridge made out of bread,
Follow the crumbs, don't lose your head.

One clue leads to a taco stand,
Where love is made with a sprinkle of sand.
A pirate's hat, a parrot's squawk,
Turns my heart into a fine autumn walk.

An 'X' marked here, near a big shoe,
Open it up, it's covered in goo!
Find the treasure, sweet as can be,
Wrapped in laughter, come share it with me.

Forget the gold, the jewels, the gems,
Give me a laugh and I'll break all the hems.
For treasure maps can lead us afar,
To the joyful moments, that's the real star.

Voices Beneath the Surface

Underneath the lake, there's quite a crowd,
Turtles sing ballads, thank you very loud.
Fishes chatter about their great fights,
Over who stole the best of the bites.

A wise old frog croaks out a tune,
Says he danced with the fireflies at noon.
But as the sunset starts to glow,
He trips on a lily, oh what a show!

The whispers of reeds tell tales quite bold,
Of a little fish who once found gold.
But the fake was a tin can, can you believe?
It celebrated fish grief, a strange way to grieve.

So listen close, the waters giggle,
With every ripple and little wiggle.
Beneath the depth, where stories flow,
Voices are laughing, putting on quite a show.

Lanterns of Legacy

In the attic lies a box of cheer,
Filled with lanterns from yesteryear.
Some flicker like the gossip untold,
While others glow with warmth so bold.

A great-grandpa's prank still lights the room,
With tales of his mustache in full bloom.
He once ran from a chicken, clear as day,
And tripped on laughter, right in the fray.

A lantern shaped like a friendly dog,
Tells of a time in a foggy bog.
Where cousins chased each other with pies,
And nothing ever really caught their eyes.

So release those lanterns, let them shine,
With funny stories that intertwine.
For in the glow of our shared delight,
A legacy lingers, always in sight.

Whispers of the Heart's Voyage

In the attic, I found a shoe,
A relic of dances, oh what a view!
Pigeons nearby chuckled with glee,
As I twirled round like a wobbly tree.

A fish took a leap, straight from the pond,
Screaming for help, quite overly fond.
But who has the time for fishy complaints?
When socks have their own gig, like odd little saints!

The cat tried to join in my big ballet,
But slipped on the floor, what a hilarious display!
He took off in fright, knocking down chairs,
Leaving me giggling with no room for cares.

And so on I danced, with the laughs all around,
In the silly old attic, joy truly found.
Each twirl made me stumble, but oh what a blast,
In my heart I knew, these moments would last.

Echoes from the Inner Sanctuary

In a cupboard, I found a great hat,
With feathers and glitter, looking quite fat.
I shoved it on, asked my dog for advice,
He rolled on the floor—so could this be nice?

A dream gave me wings made of bright spaghetti,
I soared through my kitchen like a bold confetti.
But a pot of sauce yelled, 'Not on my watch!'
So I landed quite hard, a true chef's botch!

I looked in the mirror, said, "Who's that fool?"
With noodles for hair, I broke every rule.
The jokes I could make, the laughs we could spin,
In my silly sanctuary, let the fun begin!

In echoing laughter, we danced through the night,
With two left feet, but spirits so bright.
Every giggle a treasure, each mishap a line,
In our joyful refuge, life's a grand design!

Tales Woven in Silence

Once in the woods, I whispered a joke,
To an owl who hooted, 'What's that, you bloke?'
We started a ruckus, the squirrels, they joined,
In a council of laughter, my heart was rejoined.

Each story unfolded among the tall trees,
With woodland critters, as joyful as bees.
A bear told a tale, much too grand to be true,
Of honey that tickled his toes; oh who knew?

As I sat in the shade, watching them squawk,
I jotted down tales that made my heart rock.
With crickets as music, I penned down the fun,
These silly adventures had only begun!

In the stillness of night, with twinkles so bright,
We laughed 'til we dropped, oh what a delight!
Woven in silence, these tales of the wild,
With giggles and dreams, I became a big child.

The Spirit's Unfolding Dance

With toes that go tap, and heels that go smack,
I stumbled on stage, 'Oh no!'—that's a fact.
The audience chuckled while I found my groove,
In a tumble of laughter, I began to move.

My pants took a dip, a fashion faux pas,
As I jived with a broom—now who saw that?
The janitor smiled; he knew what was up,
As I spun with delight like water from a cup.

I twirled and I whirled, what spirits do sway,
With no rhythm in mind, just pure, silly play.
A dance of mishaps, a jiggle, a hop,
My heart sang with joy, oh one could not stop!

The curtains came down, but the laughter stayed bright,
As they cheered for the dancer who danced through the night.
In every misstep, I found a new chance,
For life is a giggle, a wild, silly dance!

Timeworn Narratives

Old tales whispered in the breeze,
Laughing ghosts over trees,
Stories told by cats in hats,
Chasing shadows, dodging bats.

A grumpy grandpa's endless yarns,
About his youth and his pet barns,
With every twist, a cheeky grin,
Did he really win that race, or just spin?

Mice with dreams of becoming great,
Waltzing through crumbs, oh, what a fate!
A tale of cheese and daring thievery,
Who knew small critters could be so cleverie?

So gather round, lend an ear,
To tales that tickle, bring on the cheer,
For in each laugh, a story glows,
Time's fabric sewn with humorous prose.

Serpent's Dance of Memory

A slithering tale from days of yore,
The sneaky serpent danced on the floor,
With each twist, it forgot its place,
Leaving behind a confused face.

It hissed of treasures deep in the sand,
Where socks disappeared – wasn't that grand?
In a whirl of laughter, it lost the plot,
Now it's a legend, or so they thought.

The whispers of fish, they joined in the fun,
Telling tall tales 'til the day was done,
"Remember that time we played hide and seek?"
While the serpent just smiled, turning all chic.

Round and round, the stories flowed,
Dance of the past, a curious ode,
In every turn, a chuckle aligned,
Who knew old memories could be so blind?

Fragments of the Infinite

Once upon a time, in a world unseen,
Tea-sipping lions had quite the routine,
In a cosmic café, beyond space and time,
They'd bicker over cookies, oh so sublime.

A galactic mishap left them in stitches,
As meteors rained down like funny glitches,
"Pass the cream!" one lion did roar,
While dodging a comet that crashed by the door.

In fragments of tales, they shared every sip,
Dreaming of worlds where they'd never trip,
With each little laugh, they spun tales anew,
Of galactic cats who brewed stellar stew.

So raise your cups to the infinite fun,
Where stories collide like rays of the sun,
In every fragment, a giggle remains,
Magical moments swirling in lanes.

Heart's Compass Through Time

With a compass that spins just for kicks,
I wandered through ages, picking up tricks,
Through cavemen drawing with their toes,
To disco nights in loud sequined clothes.

I asked a knight why he carried that sword,
He mumbled something about going 'adored,'
While juggling his lance, he tripped on the ground,
And laughter erupted, the best kind around.

Then to a future where robots play chess,
They taught me the art of a well-hidden mess,
"Just blow a fuse, and you're free for the day,"
They chuckled and winked as they whirred away.

So here I stand with tales in my pack,
A heart full of humor, no story I lack,
Through ages and giggles, I'll find my way,
With a compass of chuckles to guide my play.

Crystals of Consciousness

In a crystal shop, oh what a sight,
Gems wink and glimmer, a pure delight.
One claimed to make me a better cook,
But my soup exploded—what a shady nook!

Amethyst told me to chill and just be,
While quartz tried to teach me how to be free.
But when they chimed, my cat lost her cool,
She scampered away, declaring them fools!

Turquoise said it could sing me a tune,
But all that I heard was a farting balloon.
I laughed and I danced, all crystal-wise,
Who knew enlightenment would come with such pies?

So cheers to these stones, with humor so grand,
They tickle my mind, like a quick sleight of hand.
With laughter, they whisper, they sparkle, they gleam,
In this wild, merry dance, we all share a dream!

Murmurs of the Quiet Mind

In my mind's quiet corners, giggles reside,
Thoughts bubble up like they're trying to hide.
Like rabbits in hats, they jump out with glee,
But whispers turn to chuckles, oh what a spree!

Meditation was planned, peaceful and sweet,
Yet my brain threw a party, a wild upbeat.
The thoughts wore party hats, danced on the floor,
While I just sat back, thinking 'What's the score?'

One thought said, 'Hey, let's go for a ride!'
Next thing I knew, I was caught in the tide.
With laughter echoing through each little nook,
I realized my mind's the best comedy book!

So when silence approaches, bring snacks and a drink,
For the quiet is laughter, it's more than you think.
In the depths of my head, joy bubbles like wine,
And in murmur and giggle, my thoughts intertwine!

Journeys Through the Ether

Floating through ether, on a cloud of delight,
I found a lost sock in the starry night.
It whispered of journeys, of places to roam,
But really just wanted to get back to home.

With cosmic maps drawn in crayon and glee,
I set off with a mouse, who agreed to flee.
Through dimensions of cheese and rivers of cream,
Each twist and each turn turned our giggles to steam!

We saw cosmic cats painting stars on the sea,
Who argued if the fish were swimming or free.
In space, even socks are quite wily and wise,
Through journeys of jokes, I reached for the skies!

So onward we traveled, through funny and bright,
In the ether we laughed, sparking joy through the night.
For every wild journey brings laughter and cheer,
And a sock in the cosmos brings love ever near!

Embracing the Unwritten

In pages of life, unwritten and bare,
I scribble my giggles, with wild, frizzy hair.
Each blank line winks, like a mischievous cat,
'What's your story?' it purrs, with a teasing pat.

I tried to write wisdom, oh what a feat,
But doodles of donuts and tacos took seat.
My pen rolled in laughter, the ink burst in glee,
With a heart made of giggles, who needed a decree?

So I jotted down moments, both silly and rare,
Like sloths in pajamas, or dancing with flair.
Embracing the unwritten, I found much delight,
In stories of laughter that danced through the night!

So let the pages fill with joy and with fun,
Each unwritten tale is a race to be won.
For in every story, there's laughter, it seems,
In the embraces of whimsy, we live out our dreams!

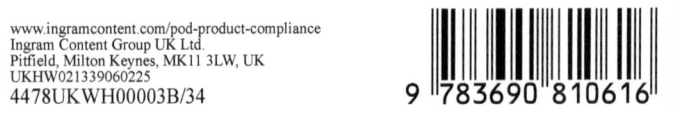